EMMANUEL JOSEPH

Constant Company Expansion (CCE) Guideline

Copyright © 2025 by Emmanuel Joseph

All rights reserved. No part of this publication may be reproduced, stored or transmitted in any form or by any means, electronic, mechanical, photocopying, recording, scanning, or otherwise without written permission from the publisher. It is illegal to copy this book, post it to a website, or distribute it by any other means without permission.

First edition

This book was professionally typeset on Reedsy. Find out more at reedsy.com

Contents

1. Chapter 1 — 1
2. Chapter 1: Foundations of Business Analysis — 2
3. Chapter 2: Identifying Business Needs and Opportunities — 4
4. Chapter 3: Gathering and Analyzing Data — 5
5. Chapter 4: Developing Solutions and Strategies — 6
6. Chapter 5: Stakeholder Engagement and Communication — 7
7. Chapter 6: Implementing Business Solutions — 9
8. Chapter 7: Monitoring and Measuring Performance — 10
9. Chapter 8: Leveraging Technology for Business Analysis — 11
10. Chapter 9: Business Analysis in Different Industries — 12
11. Chapter 10: Building a High-Performing Analysis Team — 13
12. Chapter 11: Case Studies and Real-World Examples — 14
13. Chapter 12: The Future of Business Analysis — 16

Chapter 1

Introduction

"Profit Pathways: Mastering Business Analysis for Sustainable Growth" is your comprehensive guide to understanding and applying business analysis for enduring success. This book takes you through the foundational concepts and methodologies, starting with the basics and building up to advanced techniques. Each chapter is crafted to provide you with both theoretical knowledge and practical insights. You'll explore how businesses have historically used analysis to drive growth and how modern practices are shaping the future. The book emphasizes ethical considerations, stakeholder engagement, and the critical role of innovation in business strategy.

Throughout the chapters, you'll find detailed discussions on identifying business needs, gathering and analyzing data, and developing effective solutions. The book stresses the importance of both internal and external analysis, offering tools and techniques like SWOT and PESTLE analysis, as well as real-world examples to illustrate their application. You'll also learn about the role of technology in business analysis, with insights into emerging trends and innovations that can provide your business with a competitive edge. Each chapter is designed to build your skills progressively, ensuring that you gain a comprehensive understanding of business analysis.

2

Chapter 1: Foundations of Business Analysis

Understanding the fundamentals of business analysis is the first step to mastering it. This chapter dives into the core concepts, methodologies, and principles that underpin the discipline. Business analysis is more than just crunching numbers; it's about interpreting data to make strategic decisions. We will explore key terms and frameworks, offering a solid foundation for both novices and seasoned professionals.

From the historical evolution of business analysis to modern-day practices, this chapter provides a comprehensive overview. We will examine how businesses have leveraged analysis to drive growth and sustain success. By understanding the past, we can better predict future trends and prepare for them. Emphasis will be placed on the importance of context and the role of business analysts in various industries.

The chapter will also introduce the main tools and techniques used in business analysis. From SWOT analysis to PESTLE analysis, readers will gain insight into the practical applications of these methodologies. Each tool will be explained in detail, with real-world examples to illustrate their effectiveness.

Finally, we will discuss the ethical considerations in business analysis. It's crucial for analysts to conduct their work with integrity and respect for data privacy. By adhering to ethical standards, we not only uphold the reputation of the profession but also ensure that our analyses are fair and unbiased.

3

Chapter 2: Identifying Business Needs and Opportunities

In this chapter, we shift our focus to identifying business needs and opportunities. The ability to pinpoint these aspects is critical for any successful business analysis. We will explore various techniques for uncovering unmet needs and potential areas for growth.

Understanding the market is a key component of identifying opportunities. This chapter will delve into market research methods, competitive analysis, and customer feedback. By gathering and analyzing this data, businesses can better understand their position in the market and identify areas for improvement.

Internal analysis is just as important as external research. We will discuss methods for assessing a company's strengths, weaknesses, and resources. This internal perspective helps businesses identify opportunities for optimization and innovation.

The chapter concludes with a discussion on strategic thinking. By integrating the insights gained from both internal and external analyses, businesses can develop strategies that align with their goals and drive sustainable growth. We will provide frameworks and case studies to illustrate how strategic thinking can transform business opportunities into actionable plans.

4

Chapter 3: Gathering and Analyzing Data

Data is the lifeblood of business analysis. This chapter covers the various methods and tools for gathering and analyzing data effectively. We will start with data collection techniques, including surveys, interviews, and observation. Each method has its strengths and limitations, and we will explore how to choose the most appropriate one for different scenarios.

Once data is collected, the next step is to analyze it. We will discuss statistical methods, data visualization tools, and qualitative analysis techniques. By transforming raw data into meaningful insights, businesses can make informed decisions that drive growth and success.

The chapter will also address common challenges in data analysis, such as data quality issues and biases. We will provide practical solutions for overcoming these obstacles and ensuring that analyses are accurate and reliable.

Finally, we will explore the role of technology in data analysis. From advanced analytics software to machine learning algorithms, technology is revolutionizing how we analyze data. We will discuss the latest trends and innovations, and how businesses can leverage these tools to gain a competitive edge.

5

Chapter 4: Developing Solutions and Strategies

After gathering and analyzing data, the next step is to develop solutions and strategies. This chapter provides a framework for translating insights into actionable plans. We will discuss various approaches to problem-solving and decision-making, including root cause analysis and the 5 Whys technique.

Innovation is a key theme in this chapter. We will explore how businesses can foster a culture of innovation and creativity, encouraging employees to think outside the box. By developing innovative solutions, businesses can address challenges and seize new opportunities.

Strategic planning is also crucial for sustainable growth. We will discuss the components of a successful strategic plan, including setting objectives, defining key performance indicators (KPIs), and creating action plans. Case studies will be used to illustrate how strategic planning can drive business success.

The chapter concludes with a discussion on implementation and monitoring. Developing a strategy is only the first step; it must be effectively implemented and continuously monitored to ensure success. We will provide tips and best practices for ensuring that strategies are executed smoothly and achieve the desired outcomes.

6

Chapter 5: Stakeholder Engagement and Communication

Effective communication and stakeholder engagement are critical for successful business analysis. This chapter explores strategies for engaging stakeholders, from executives to frontline employees. We will discuss the importance of understanding stakeholder needs and expectations and how to address them effectively.

Building strong relationships with stakeholders requires excellent communication skills. We will provide tips and techniques for clear and persuasive communication, including storytelling and active listening. By effectively communicating analysis findings and recommendations, businesses can gain buy-in and support for their initiatives.

The chapter also covers the role of collaboration in business analysis. We will explore methods for fostering a collaborative environment, where stakeholders are actively involved in the analysis process. By working together, businesses can leverage diverse perspectives and expertise to develop more effective solutions.

Finally, we will discuss the importance of transparency and trust in stakeholder engagement. By being open and honest about analysis methods, findings, and limitations, businesses can build trust and credibility with their stakeholders. This trust is essential for fostering long-term relationships and achieving sustainable growth.

7

Chapter 6: Implementing Business Solutions

This chapter focuses on the practical aspects of implementing business solutions. We will discuss the steps involved in turning strategic plans into actionable projects, including project management techniques and best practices. Effective implementation requires careful planning, coordination, and execution.

Change management is a key theme in this chapter. Implementing new solutions often involves significant changes to processes, systems, and behaviors. We will explore strategies for managing change, including communication, training, and support. By effectively managing change, businesses can minimize resistance and ensure a smooth transition.

The chapter also covers risk management. We will discuss methods for identifying, assessing, and mitigating risks associated with implementing business solutions. By proactively addressing potential risks, businesses can increase the likelihood of successful implementation.

Finally, we will provide case studies and examples of successful implementations. These real-world examples will illustrate the challenges and best practices associated with implementing business solutions. By learning from the experiences of others, businesses can increase their chances of success.

8

Chapter 7: Monitoring and Measuring Performance

Once solutions are implemented, it is crucial to monitor and measure their performance. This chapter explores methods for tracking progress and evaluating the effectiveness of business solutions. We will discuss key performance indicators (KPIs), metrics, and dashboards.

Regular monitoring allows businesses to identify issues and make necessary adjustments. We will provide tips and best practices for setting up effective monitoring systems. By continuously tracking performance, businesses can ensure that they are on the right path to achieving their goals.

The chapter also covers the role of feedback in performance measurement. We will discuss methods for gathering feedback from stakeholders, including surveys, interviews, and focus groups. By actively seeking feedback, businesses can gain valuable insights and make informed decisions.

Finally, we will explore the importance of continuous improvement. Business analysis is an ongoing process, and it is essential to continually refine and optimize solutions. We will provide strategies for fostering a culture of continuous improvement, where businesses are always looking for ways to enhance their performance and achieve sustainable growth.

9

Chapter 8: Leveraging Technology for Business Analysis

Technology plays a crucial role in modern business analysis. This chapter explores the various tools and technologies available to business analysts, from advanced analytics software to artificial intelligence (AI) and machine learning (ML) algorithms.

We will discuss the benefits and challenges of leveraging technology in business analysis. Technology can provide powerful insights and efficiencies, but it also requires careful planning and management. We will provide tips and best practices for selecting and implementing the right tools for your business.

The chapter also covers emerging trends and innovations in technology. We will explore how businesses can stay ahead of the curve by adopting the latest technologies and staying informed about industry developments. By leveraging technology, businesses can gain a competitive edge and drive sustainable growth.

Finally, we will provide case studies and examples of businesses that have successfully leveraged technology in their analysis processes. These real-world examples will illustrate the potential of technology to transform business analysis and drive success.

10

Chapter 9: Business Analysis in Different Industries

Business analysis is a versatile discipline that can be applied in various industries. This chapter explores how business analysis techniques can be adapted to different sectors, from healthcare to finance to retail.

We will discuss the unique challenges and opportunities associated with each industry. By understanding the specific context and requirements of different sectors, business analysts can tailor their approaches to achieve the best results.

The chapter also covers industry-specific tools and techniques. We will provide examples of how different industries leverage business analysis to drive growth and success. By learning from these examples, businesses can gain valuable insights and apply them to their own contexts.

Finally, we will explore the role of industry regulations and standards in business analysis. Compliance with industry-specific regulations is crucial for ensuring that analyses are accurate, reliable, and ethical. We will discuss best practices for staying compliant and maintaining the highest standards of professionalism.

11

Chapter 10: Building a High-Performing Analysis Team

A successful business analysis effort requires a high-performing team. This chapter explores the key elements of building and managing an effective analysis team, from recruitment to training to leadership.

We will discuss the skills and competencies required for business analysts. By understanding the attributes of successful analysts, businesses can better identify and develop talent within their organizations.

Team dynamics and collaboration are also crucial for success. We will explore strategies for fostering a collaborative environment, where team members can share ideas, learn from each other, and work together to achieve common goals.

The chapter concludes with a discussion on leadership and management. Effective leadership is essential for guiding and motivating analysis teams. We will provide tips and best practices for leading analysis teams, from setting clear goals to providing ongoing support and feedback.

12

Chapter 11: Case Studies and Real-World Examples

This chapter provides a collection of case studies and real-world examples to illustrate the concepts discussed in previous chapters. We will examine businesses from various industries and analyze how they have successfully implemented business analysis techniques to drive growth and sustainability.

Each case study will detail the specific challenges faced by the business, the analysis methods used, and the solutions developed. We will also discuss the outcomes and lessons learned from each example. By studying these real-world scenarios, readers can gain practical insights and inspiration for their own business analysis efforts.

The chapter will cover a diverse range of industries, including technology, healthcare, finance, and retail. We will highlight the unique approaches taken by each business and how they adapted their strategies to their specific contexts. This variety will demonstrate the versatility and applicability of business analysis across different sectors.

Finally, we will provide a framework for conducting your own case studies. By systematically analyzing real-world examples, businesses can continually learn and improve their analysis processes. This ongoing learning is crucial for achieving sustainable growth and staying competitive in a rapidly

CHAPTER 11: CASE STUDIES AND REAL-WORLD EXAMPLES

changing business environment.

13

Chapter 12: The Future of Business Analysis

The final chapter looks ahead to the future of business analysis. We will explore emerging trends and technologies that are shaping the field, from big data and advanced analytics to artificial intelligence and machine learning.

We will discuss the opportunities and challenges associated with these trends. While new technologies can provide powerful insights and efficiencies, they also require careful planning and management. We will provide tips and best practices for staying ahead of the curve and leveraging these innovations to drive business success.

The chapter also covers the evolving role of business analysts. As the field continues to grow and change, analysts must adapt and expand their skill sets. We will discuss the importance of continuous learning and professional development, and provide resources for staying informed about industry developments.

Finally, we will reflect on the broader implications of business analysis for society and the economy. By driving sustainable growth and innovation, business analysis can contribute to a more prosperous and equitable world. We will conclude with a call to action for readers to embrace the principles of business analysis and use them to make a positive impact in their own organizations and communities.

Conclusion

As you reach the final chapters, "Profit Pathways" provides a forward-looking perspective on the future of business analysis. You'll gain insights into how technological advancements like artificial intelligence and machine learning are revolutionizing the field. The book also emphasizes the importance of continuous improvement and professional development to keep pace with industry changes. You'll explore case studies and real-world examples that demonstrate the practical application of concepts discussed, helping you to translate theory into action.

The concluding chapters offer a call to action, encouraging you to leverage the principles of business analysis to make a positive impact in your organization and community. By fostering a culture of innovation, ethical practices, and strategic thinking, you can drive sustainable growth and achieve long-term success. "Profit Pathways" is not just a guide; it's a blueprint for mastering business analysis and using it as a powerful tool to navigate the complex landscape of modern business.

www.ingramcontent.com/pod-product-compliance
Lightning Source LLC
LaVergne TN
LVHW020509080526
838202LV00057B/6268